EUR.P.DES.
BEECHE

DRAMA CLASSICS *the first hundred*

The Alchemist
All for Love
Andromache
Antigone
Arden of Faversham
Bacchae
Bartholomew Fair
The Beaux Stratagem
The Beggar's Opera
Birds
The Changeling
A Chaste Maid in
    Cheapside
The Cherry Orchard
Children of the Sun
El Cid
The Country Wife
Cyrano de Bergerac
The Dance of Death
The Devil is an
    Ass
Doctor Faustus
A Doll's House
Don Juan
The Duchess of
    Malfi
Edward II
Electra (Euripides)
Electra (Sophocles)
An Enemy of the
    People
Every Man in his
    Humour
Everyman
The Father
Faust
A Flea in her Ear
Frogs
Fuenteovejuna
The Game of Love
    and Chance

Ghosts
The Government
    Inspector
Hedda Gabler
The Hypochondriac
The Importance of
    Being Earnest
An Ideal Husband
An Italian Straw Hat
The Jew of Malta
The Knight of the
    Burning Pestle
The Lady from the Sea
The Learned Ladies
Life is a Dream
The Lower Depths
The Lucky Chance
Lulu
Lysistrata
The Magistrate
The Malcontent
The Man of Mode
The Marriage of Figaro
Mary Stuart
The Master Builder
Medea
The Misanthrope
The Miser
Miss Julie
A Month in the
    Country
A New Way to Pay
    Old Debts
Oedipus at Kolonos
Oedipus the King
The Oresteia
Peer Gynt
Phèdre
Philoctetes
The Playboy of the
    Western World

The Recruiting
    Officer
The Revenger's
    Tragedy
The Rivals
The Roaring Girl
The Robbers
La Ronde
Rosmersholm
The Rover
The School for
    Scandal
The Seagull
The Servant of Two
    Masters
She Stoops to Conquer
The Shoemaker's
    Holiday
The Spanish Tragedy
Spring's Awakening
Tartuffe
Thérèse Raquin
Three Sisters
'Tis Pity She's a
    Whore
Too Clever by Half
Ubu
Uncle Vanya
Vassa Zheleznova
Volpone
The Way of the World
The White Devil
The Wild Duck
Women Beware
    Women
Women of Troy
Woyzeck

*The publishers welcome
suggestions for further titles*

DRAMA CLASSICS

BACCHAE

by

Euripides

translated and with an introduction by
Frederic Raphael and Kenneth McLeish

NICK HERN BOOKS

London

www.nickhernbooks.co.uk

A Drama Classic

Bacchae first published in Great Britain in this translation
as a paperback original in 1998 by Nick Hern Books Limited,
14 Larden Road, London W3 7ST

Reprinted 2000

Copyright in this translation © 1998
Volatic Ltd and Kenneth McLeish

Copyright in the introduction © 1998 Nick Hern Books

Typeset by Country Setting, Kingsdown, Kent CT14 8ES
Printed by Athenaeum Press Ltd, Gateshead, Tyne and Wear

A CIP catalogue record for this book is available from
the British Library

ISBN 1 85459 411 7

Introduction

Euripides

Euripides was born either in 485 BC or 480 BC, and
died in 406 BC. He was a wealthy man: his family owned
property on the island of Salamis (where, legend has it,
he used to work in a remote cave fitted out as a writing-
room). His first play was produced when he was about
30, and he went on to write 92 plays altogether, of
which nineteen survive. The size of the corpus that
has come down to us, a dozen more than from either
Aeschylus or Sophocles, is a tribute to Euripides'
popularity not so much in his own time as later, when
the manuscripts were copied. For over 2000 years he
was the best known, most admired and most influential
of all Greek dramatists.

If Euripides' surviving plays are good evidence, he was
less interested in 'verbal music' than were either Aeschylus
or Sophocles. His language is seldom 'sublime'; lines
justify themselves by their place in the dramatic logic,
by what they contribute to the flow of ideas and
confrontations. He proceeds not with the mellifluous
majesty of an Aeschylus or the solemn moral grandeur
of a Sophocles, but by a torrent of dialectic, by abrupt
turns and clashes of character, by visual and conceptual
coups de théâtre. He is outstanding at showing characters

in states of emotional and psychological stress, and he manipulates each situation, each myth, to do so.

Euripides' combination of intensity and philosophical insight can be disconcerting: his revisionist approach to the ancient myths and his sceptical attitudes both to the Olympian gods and to the political orthodoxies of Periclean Athens reflect the 'advanced' thinking of his time as well as, no doubt, personal insight. His high reputation came very largely after his death. In his lifetime his plays seldom won first prizes, at the height of his career he was prosecuted (unsuccessfully) for impiety, and in his seventies, controversial and unregenerate to the last, he was forced to flee from 'democratic' Athens to monarchical Macedonia.

Bacchae: **What Happens in the Play**

Before the royal palace of Thebes, the god Dionysos appears. He explains how he was born miraculously in the city, but was rejected by the people. He has now returned, and intends to make all Thebes accept him, beginning with the women, whom he has filled with ecstasy and driven into the mountains. He disappears to join them there, on Mount Kithairon, and the Chorus enters, singing and dancing in his honour, telling key parts of his myth, and describing how his ecstatic worshippers, the Bacchae ('bacchants') or Maenads ('ecstatic ones'), dance like foals frisking in his honour.

Two old men, the prophet Teiresias and Kadmos, former king of Thebes, enter dressed as Maenads. They are planning to go and join the dance, but are interrupted by King Pentheus. He is furious that the women have been hoodwinked by a 'pretty boy', a charlatan. He has arrested and imprisoned them, and is proposing to do the same to Dionysos. Teiresias tries to convince him that the 'charlatan' is God, and advises acceptance. But Pentheus sends his guards to find Dionysos. The Chorus sings of its devotion to the god and its outrage at the way Pentheus is treating him. Then Dionysos is brought in, bound. The guard-commander tells how the women have miraculously escaped from prison, and how Dionysos willingly accepted arrest, smiling and holding out his hands as if to welcome the binding-ropes. Left alone, Pentheus questions Dionysos, refuses to accept his assurance that he is (or knows) God, and sends him to prison.

The Chorus begins another dance of indignation and bewilderment. It is interrupted by Dionysos' voice, calling from the prison, and by a bolt of lightning which sets the palace ablaze. Dionysos appears to his followers – and Pentheus runs out angrily after him. Before they can quarrel, a cowherd hurries in from Mount Kithairon. He tells of the women, high in the hills: peaceful, placid, then raging with God's ecstasy till they hunt down and kill any animal in their path, and finally at peace again. Pentheus vows to punish them, and Dionysos suddenly changes character. Playing on the king's desire to spy on the women at their secret ritual, he persuades him to disguise himself as a woman and hide in the trees where he can see but not be seen. Pentheus goes in to change clothes, and the Chorus sings of what 'wisdom' is, and of the punishment suffered by mortals who mistake its nature.

Pentheus appears, dressed as a Bacchant, and Dionysos leads him, as if in a daze, away to Mount Kithairon. After a choral dance of anger against the 'unbeliever', an attendant stumbles in, shaking with terror. He tells how the God and the King came to the mountain, how Dionysos bent a fir-tree to the ground, put Pentheus in the high branches, then revealed him to the Bacchae as a climbing beast, a spy. They uprooted the tree, tore Pentheus to pieces and played catch with his limbs. Now they are coming in procession back to Thebes, led by Agave, Pentheus' aged mother, with his head impaled on her *thyrsos* (sacred staff). The last part of the play (originally, mainly musical) begins with a chorus of joy at Pentheus' punishment. Agave and the Bacchae enter, rejoicing at the 'lion they danced to death'. But then Kadmos comes in, with servants bringing the remains of Pentheus' body. He shocks Agave out of her trance, and shows her what she has in her hands, and what she has done. Dionysos appears on high, and announces that Thebes' punishment is complete for rejecting him. Broken-hearted and bewildered (how could God do this?'), Agave and Kadmos stumble out to exile, and the play ends with the bleak choral reflection that God is not to be understood or challenged, that mortal hopes are vain and that all we can do, when the supernatural enters our lives, is 'expect the unexpected'.

Bacchae

Bacchae was first performed in 405 BC, a few months after Euripides' death in exile at the Macedonian court. In the following year, 404 BC, the 27-year Peloponnesian War came at last to an end, Athens accepted humiliating peace-terms; in the reign of austerity and censorship imposed by the victorious Spartans, theatre productions dwindled almost to nothing. The great age of Athenian tragedy was over.

At first sight, *Bacchae* seems unlike any other of Euripides' surviving plays. It avoids direct political, moral and ethical comment, of the kind common in, say, *Women of Troy* (savage about the effects of war), *Medea* (outspoken about the relationship between men and women) or *Orestes* (with its reflections on family duty and social obligation). It contains none of the awkward questions Euripides asked in other plays about religious belief, for example 'If all we see around us is disaster and suffering, why should we think God cares for us?' (*Hecuba*), or 'What do we do if we think that the God we believe in is a tyrant and a criminal?' (*Ion*). In fact it seems free of questions and comments altogether: the self-contained presentation of a simple dramatic situation, without diversions or irrelevances. God comes, reveals himself and punishes those who refuse to accept him.

As always with Euripides, however, simplicity of style and surface mask far greater complexity. The questions and comments in *Bacchae* are no less sharp for being latent. The cult which overwhelms the Thebans in the play may be religious, but Euripides' picture of communal panic and bewilderment must also have had political resonance in the last, flailing months of the Peloponnesian War. The play's tight focus on a single dilemma, a single tragedy, leaves a question unspoken but noisy in the air:

'If this horror is the present, what will the future be and however will we cope with it?' The play ends not with resolution of the conflict between Dionysos and Pentheus, but with Agave's and Kadmos' agonised realisation that despite everything they have believed and suffered until now, tomorrow is unpredictable, imminent and inevitable.

In a way quite different from Aeschylus or Sophocles (who pose ethical and philosophical questions in ways which imply clear answers), Euripides leaves the issues hanging, for each member of the audience to resolve in his or her own way. And in *Bacchae*, in a manner familiar from his earlier plays, he relates his hard questions to a myth of the most bizarre and uncompromising kind. Dionysos and the cult which engulfs the characters in this play are not comfortable or predictable, they are wild, absurd, irrational – and stand utterly outside the whole pattern of Theban life till now. Ever since Dionysos' extraordinary birth – to a woman made pregnant by a thunderbolt – the Thebans have tried to forget him. They have built an edifice of custom and usage, a 'civilisation', which excludes the awkwardness and irrationality which Dionysos symbolises: that is, what the French philosopher Rousseau was later to call 'the Beast in Man'. And then Dionysos reappears and invites them, forcefully and irresistibly, to re-examine both the edifice they have made of their lives and their own underlying natures. The challenge is as exhilarating as it is terrifying – and it reflects a common Euripidean theme, that God's demands on us are objective, and it is by the way we react to those demands that we discover who we are.

Dionysos was the god of the moment of surrender to impulse or events, the abandonment of rational control. In all human actions, the Greeks believed, there was a moment when you were still in control and could pull back from what you planned; beyond that moment there was no return. A soldier about to kill someone could stop himself – but only up to the moment of no alternative. A word of anger or love could be checked – until the very last instant before it was uttered. In belief, there was a hinge moment when irrational faith took over from ordered thought. Dionysos was the god of all such moments. His worshippers believed that only the gods enjoyed a perfect balance between reason and instinct, and that Dionysos allowed human beings momentary glimpses of that perfection in their own lives, in the same way that wine (his gift to mortals) allowed them a small taste of the nectar drunk by the gods, and (in the heady instant before control was replaced by drunkenness) a fleeting taste of the eternal life which nectar gave the gods.

To modern readers and spectators, brought up in faith-cultures alien to those of ancient Greece, the forms which Dionysos-worship took can seem absurd. (They may also have seemed so to the ultra-rational Athenians of Euripides' own time – and he certainly spares us, and his contemporaries, none of their terrible 'otherness'.) In common with many other mystery-religions – Mithra-ism and Isis-worship are examples – the Dionysos-ritual required its adherents metaphorically to shed their human identity and turn into animals. The cowherd in this play describes the process exactly (pages 32-5). The women are in the high mountain-pastures, placid and at peace. Then, without warning, the god calls them and they become like hunting-dogs, racing frenziedly up and down, tearing to pieces anything in their path. As soon as the ecstasy passes, they return to their serene, pre-frenzied state: all is as it was, and yet everything has changed.

If there is strangeness here, it is the strangeness not merely of the Dionysos-cult but of all religious action. Whirling dervishes, fakirs gashing themselves with blades, Pentecostal Christians speaking in tongues, monks and mystics practising austerities which take them closer to their gods – all operate on a level which similarly involves both a surrender of rationality and a return to a 'normality' which the fulfilment of the ritual has forever changed. Pentheus' failing in this play is not that he is blind and wants to see (that is, to accept); he is blind and wants to *spy*. In a fundamentalist cult there is no room for outsiders, you accept or stay away. But Euripides is also interested in those who join a cult, accept its teaching and are then forced to stand back and face themselves. Agonisingly, they return to their 'rational' lives in the full knowledge both of what transcendental ecstasy is like, and of its potential to destroy as well as to delight.

For some readers and spectators, *Bacchae* remains a political allegory. They say that surrender to Dionysos stands for surrender to the ecstasy of war, and that the choices and fate of each of the play's human characters (Kadmos, Agave, Teiresias, Pentheus, the soldiers and the servants) have parallels in the real Athenian world outside the theatre. Perhaps Euripides' spectators, or some of them, also thought such thoughts in the dying days of 'the glory that was Athens', perhaps such thoughts are common in all 'civilised' societies threatened by an irrational and overwhelming outside force. For others, however, such explanations are only part of the play's meaning. It is an examination of our species' whole need to accept the inexplicable, and of the ways we organise ourselves to do so. And the play's continuing relevance, 2500 years after it was written, not to mention its extraordinary ability simultaneously to exhilarate and discomfort anyone who takes it even remotely seriously, reflects not merely Euripides' mastery but also the bitter continuity in human life of political and religious tyrannies and absurdities of every kind, from Roman religious persecution to Nazism, from Holy Wars to millennial cults of every degree of dottiness and barbarism.

Dionysos

Dionysos is both the most 'human' and the most unpredictable of the Greek gods. He is unique among the Olympians in having had a mortal mother: Semele, daughter of Kadmos, the founder of Thebes. Zeus usually disguised himself before coupling with mortal women (for instance, as a swan when he mated with Leda). At Semele's demand, however, Zeus displayed himself to her in all his electric majesty. Semele died of the shock, but – thanks to Zeus' ingenuity – her child survived and became immortal. Zeus hid the embryo from Hera, his official wife, by sewing it into his thigh until the infant came to term. As soon as Dionysos was born, he used his supernatural power to go down to Hades, reclaim his mother, and instal her among the Olympians.

Dionysos grew to be a god who could not be controlled. He took all limitations as an affront. He straddled the gulf between male and female, civilisation and barbarism, pleasure and pain. He neither respected 'normal' boundaries nor inspired routine prudence. Unlike Apollo, whose lyre calmed his followers, Dionysos' favourite instrument was the pipe, which excited the dance and prompted excess. Like a rock musician, he was the storming outsider who made decent people shudder; Zeus' dangerous thunder rumbled on in him.

It was tempting for traditional scholars to regard Dionysos as alien to the Greek pantheon. He was often said to have been an eccentric newcomer from Lydia or Thrace, where his orgiastic cults were current; they survive in the travesty weddings of modern Greek folklore. He was particularly honoured at Athens. In March/April a regular Dionysiac procession brought him from Eleutherai ('Freetown'), in the mountains near Boeotia, the region of which Thebes was the capital. The procession culminated in the inauguration of the theatrical season when Athens was home to competitions, comic and tragic, in honour of the god. At these competitions, the pious and unsmiling formality of tragedy was spiced by satyr plays and comedies in which gods and heroes degenerated from intimidating powers into objects of derision. (Laughter and horror were never as far apart in the Greek theatre as Aristotle classified them.)

Dionysos was both the presiding patron of the theatre and also a god who liked to play the part of the strolling, or cavorting, player: it always amused him to impersonate the Outsider. As was the case with the hero Odysseus,

cunning intelligence was one of Dionysos' cardinal
attributes: he was as sly as he was changeable. In *Bacchae*
he adopts the weakness of an apparently effeminate
adolescent in order to work the *coups de théâtre* which are
his speciality. On another occasion, when abducted by
pirates, he caused their ship to turn into a waterborne
jungle. He himself became a lion who consumed the
captain and then made the crew leap into the water
where, by a rare act of grace, they were frisked into
dolphins.

Dionysos' errant genius was celebrated by the fact that
the theatres where he was honoured were his only temples.
As far as worship goes, he enjoyed the least grandiose of
worshippers. His *thiasos* or congregation, met in the open;
wherever they planted their (may)pole, crowned with a
mask, became a temporary place of worship. Lacking
regular priests, he was sometimes represented by a *xoanon*
or wooden effigy, one of the earliest forms of divine
'statue'. It had to be carried by a female devotee who
had herself been carried away, like the Bacchae in
Euripides' play, by the black flame of mystic madness.

Dionysos was not only the god of fruitfulness, of moisture,
of overflowing life, and the apostle of pleasure, he is also
linked with death, which gives life its meaning. His cult
took ecstasy to the threshold of murder, and across it: the
tearing apart and eating of a living animal, contrary to
the usages of Greek civility, announced his followers'
return to 'nature' in its most savage form. In *Bacchae,* in
a typically Euripidean twist, it is Pentheus' own god-
possessed mother Agave who solicits her fellow-Maenads
to dismember the son whom, in her possessed state, she

fails to recognise. The one person in the world who might have been expected to be his protector instigates her offspring's destruction: ecstatic femininity has passions, not loyalties.

Original Staging

Bacchae was first produced in the Theatre of Dionysos, outside the god's shrine at the foot of the Acropolis in Athens. It was part of a competitive religious and dramatic festival, before a (mainly male) audience of some 14,000 people. Each playwright directed his plays (three or four, on a single day), arranged the choreography and perhaps composed the music; some playwrights also acted. There were three actors, all male and all masked; apart from the fact that the first actor played Dionysos, there is no information on how the parts in *Bacchae* were allocated. A Chorus of fifteen, all male, sang and danced; its leader also took part in the spoken dialogue. (Unlike the actors, who were professionals, these Chorus-members were amateurs, boys and men chosen by lot, one from each main district of the city. It was an honour to appear at the Festival, both for the individual himself and for the district he represented.) There were also (silent) attendants and an unknown number of musicians, probably playing flute, lyre, drum and cymbal or tambourine.

Something like one third of *Bacchae* was declaimed or sung with instrumental accompaniment and formal movement. The rhythms were organised not by stress, as in English verse, but by 'quantity': that is, the lines were arranged in patterns of 'long' and 'short' syllables, depending on the

length of the vowel-sounds. These patterns also deter-
mined the rhythms of the music and the dance-steps.
The choruses frequently used *strophe* and *antistrophe*, the
rhythm of one section exactly repeating that of the lines
before. The music was in single overlapping lines without
harmony, in the manner we now associate with Middle
Eastern or Far Eastern music. The verse moves between
speech (usually in resolved iambics, analogous to loose
English blank verse) and declamation or song (usually in
the more complex rhythmic patterns known as 'lyric'
metres because they were accompanied by the lyre).

A feature of this play, as of all Greek tragedy, is a number
of short ejaculations: *e, feoo, aee* and so on. Each is used
in specific circumstances, and seems to have had specific
meaning. They were probably not onomatopoeic, but
were instructions to the actors or musicians to improvise
particular kinds of vocal or musical melismas: sounds
conveying emotion without turning into words. In most
translations these ejaculations are omitted, or replaced
with such undramatic English equivalents as 'Alas!' or
'Woe!', here we have simply transliterated, leaving the
performers to interpret.

Bacchae in Myth and in Euripides

Greek tragedies were usually based on stories from the
huge corpus of myths about the gods and heroes of what
was assumed to be the real, if distant past. The word
mythos means literally 'story', but myth was also a kind of
truth from which states and individuals derived their ideas
of themselves and their genealogies. (The Athenians, for

example, went looking for the bones of their mythical king Theseus, found a hoard of fossilised remains on Aigina, and took them reverently home.) Greek theatre used the myths in much the same way as later Indian drama quarried the *Mahabharata* and *Ramayana*. The spectators would know the outline of each myth, and their interest would be in how the playwright interpreted it. His stylishness, his emphases or ironies, the slant he put on common knowledge: these factors, no less than technical invention, stagecraft and its surprises, would determine assessments of his wit or his genius, and lead both to his place in the prize-competition and to the enhancement or diminution of his literary reputation.

The basic events of *Bacchae* – Dionysos' miraculous birth, his return to Thebes and the punishment of Pentheus – would have been as familiar to the audience, in advance, as stories of Robin Hood or King Arthur are to audiences nowadays. Spectators at the original production would have the extra buzz (lost to modern audiences) of watching the play in the god's own theatre, next to his shrine in Athens, and in a festival devoted to his honour. They may well have spent the days previous to the production in watching or taking part in processions, ceremonies, musical contests and other celebrations. The atmosphere was probably a mixture of sacred solemnity and the hilarity and hysteria one might expect of any big public festival held in a town under siege in wartime.

In *Bacchae*, Euripides made full ironical use of all these circumstances. The main Dionysos-stories are plainly told, in celebratory song and dance. The issues are debated (for example by Teiresias and Pentheus or by Pentheus and Dionysos). There is knockabout (particularly with the old men) and there is horror (in the Attendant's description of Pentheus' murder). There is cathartic realisation and acceptance of suffering, presented in a large-scale musical finale. And underlying all this is a sustained and consistently surprising meditation on belief, the nature of the supernatural and the claims and counter-claims between gods and mortals. This was the Euripidean mixture ('expect the unexpected'), already familiar from pieces otherwise as disparate as *Herakles* and *Hippolytos*, *Alkestis* and *Elektra*. But few plays, even in Euripides' controversial catalogue, ever deconstructed the whole nature of the sacred festival, its rituals and its drama, and at the same time confirmed them, with such a mixture of audacious thought and breathtaking, casual-seeming technical expertise.

It is often observed that the masks of both tragedy and comedy can hang from the same peg, or idea; but here the same play can be seen – and needs to be performed – as its own double, as tragedy and comedy. Its text can be tilted to two different lights and read in contradictory senses. The horror in the play is so grotesque that it challenges the distinction between tragedy and comedy. The climax of the action is certainly terrible and – since the young king brings death on himself by his own vanity – it can almost pass for a proper instance of the *hubris* which is the traditional 'flaw' of the Greek tragic hero. Yet Pentheus' fate lacks tragic dignity. Is it worthy of a hero to be caught spying on a bunch of women while dressed in drag? Is it a noble fate to die after running like a stag from a party of crazed huntresses?

Insolent playfulness is one mood of the play throughout. The human males dress up as women, a god is cast as the protagonist of a tragedy, and Euripides further subverts conventional divinity by humanising Dionysos with sentiments of resentment. He both warns us of the ferocious capability of what lies beyond human control and dares to depict a divinity as the epitome of aggressive camp. It is his genius that he could contrive a play which is so mould-breakingly ambivalent.

Frederic Raphael, Kenneth McLeish

For Further Reading

G.M.A. Grube, *The Drama of Euripides* (*1961*) and T.B.L. Webster, *The Tragedies of Euripides* (1967) are good scholarly guides to the plays, and D.J. Conacher, *Euripidean Drama* (1967) deals well with Euripides' treatment of myth. R.P. Winnington-Ingram, *Euripides and Dionysos* (1954) is a learned but fascinating discussion of the issues raised by this particular play. Peter Arnott, *An Introduction to the Greek Theatre* (1965) gives details of how plays were performed in ancient Athens, and Mary Renault, *The Mask of Apollo* (1966) is an atmospheric historical novel set in the ancient theatre and with a convincing actor-hero.

Euripides: Key Dates

NB All dates are BC.

485   (or 480) Euripides born.

455   First play produced.

438   *Alkestis.*

431   *Medea.* Outbreak of Peloponnesian War.

428   *Hippolytos.*

415   *Women of Troy.* Athens' disastrous expedition against Syracuse in Sicily (led by, among others, Euripides' friend Alcibiades).

408   Attacked for 'impiety', went into self-exile in Macedonia.

406   Died.

405   *Bacchae* posthumously produced.

BACCHAE

Characters

DIONYSOS
PENTHEUS
TEIRESIAS
KADMOS
GUARD COMMANDER
COWHERD
ATTENDANT
AGAVE

GUARDS, ATTENDANTS (*silent parts*)

CHORUS of Bacchae

Note: Glossary and Pronunciation Guide at end of play

Thebes. An open space before PENTHEUS' *palace. First light.*
Enter DIONYSOS *on high.*

DIONYSOS.
    You see the son of God. I have returned.
    Dionysos, son of Zeus. Home, here, to Thebes.
    My mother was Semele, King Kadmos' daughter,
    My father Zeus. Lightning the midwife:
    Born in a flash, the fire-child.
    I have changed my shape: God comes in mortal guise.
    See – here by the waters of Dirke, Ismenos' stream –
    My mother's tomb, lightning-scorched,
    Still smoking, Hera's vivid rage,
    Palace and pyre. King Kadmos – honour to him –
    Declared it holy: no foot must touch it,
    His daughter's shrine. Here, too, my offering:
    A cluster of springing vines.

    My journey began in golden fields;
    Phrygia, Lydia, sun-blistered Persian plains,
    Baktria's battlements I passed,
    The wintry country of the Medes,
    Then generous Arabia, wide Asia –
    Tall-towered towns, twinned in glassy sea –
    Greeks and barbarians, clamorous community.
    All of them I quickened into dance, charged

With my mysteries. And now I come to Thebes,
First of all Greek cities. Here God appears
To mortals.

I've goaded them to ecstasy,
Decked them in fawnskins,
The thyrsos in their hands, the ivied spear.
Thebes must be first! For here
My mother's sisters – they should have known better –
Denied me. I was not the seed of Zeus:
Semele, they said, their sister, my mother,
Gave some man her virginity and laid the blame on
Zeus.
Blasphemy, they said: King Kadmos' idea,
Punished by a thunderbolt from Zeus.
They denied me, God,
And for that I've sent them mad,
Panicked them into the mountains,
Parted from their wits, animals
In ritual's savage panoply –
Yes, all the female seed of Thebes,
Every woman in the place,
And Kadmos' daughters first among all.
Wild for me they huddle, witless,
By roofless crags and shaggy pines.
This city must learn – once and for all,
Like it or not – that I am master
Of the world's dance and they must revel in it.
Prisoners of death, look up, say yes to God,
To Semele's son, the living seed of Zeus.

King Kadmos has abdicated. His throne and power
Are Pentheus' now, his daughter's son.

And Pentheus battles the God in me,
Denies me sacrifice, excludes me from his prayers.
No mercy! He'll acknowledge me God for this –
And all the Thebans too. Only then,
Rights vindicated here, will I move on
And show my majesty in other lands.
If Thebes takes sullen arms against my worshippers,
My Bacchae, tries to drive them from the mountains,
I'll lead my army at them, my maenad-force.
Why else thus clothe myself in mortal form?
Why else dress God as man?

Women! Women! You followed me
From Tmolos, breastplate of Asia,
My women, my dancers, my holy ones.
Drum now, drum, the beat I made
For Mother Earth, with Mother Earth,
Drum here, now, drum on Pentheus' walls,
Be seen! Be seen! To Kithairon now
I go, to the mountain, to lead the dance.

Exit. Enter CHORUS.

CHORUS.
Asia, Asia,
From there we crowd;
Sacred Tmolos left behind,
We come, praising Dionysos,
Sweet burden,
Dionysos, lord.

Who's listening?
Inside, out here with us?

Shrink back, bow down,
No word of doubt as I cry his name,
Over and over:
Dionysos, lord.

Happy, happy
Who brims with God,
Soul charged with God;
Who chants, who dances,
High in the hills;
Who chants her mysteries,
Kybele, Mother, Mother,
Lifts thyrsos high,
Wears ivy crown,
For Dionysos, lord.

Come Bacchae, come Bacchae –
Dance him here, the roaring boy,
Dionysos, God son of God,
God son of Zeus.
Dance him from Phrygia's hills,
Dance him through all the ways of Greece,
Your Dionysos, dance.

Dionysos, lord!
She carried him. She bore him,
Racked by lightning
Before her time was due,
His birth her death,
Torn by the thunderbolt.

Then Zeus, Zeus, a second womb,
Hid child in godly thigh,

Pinned tight with golden pins
Safe hidden from Hera, queen.
And then, when the Fates decreed,
Gave him second birth,
Bull-horned, snake-crowned.
So now his worshippers, his dancers,
Snatch living snakes,
Wear crowns of snakes.

Thebes, Thebes,
Where Semele was born,
Wear ivy crowns,
Wear briony –
Green tendrils, berries white.
Oak spears, fir spears,
Dappled fawnskins
Crown them, tufts, white wool.

The thyrsos, proud, erect –
Worship it, worship it!
Earth shudders, dances.
Dionysos herds us
To the mountain, the mountain.
There they throng, the women,
Spindles forgotten, looms,
In rut for Dionysos.

God-guarded cave of Crete,
Secret womb where Zeus was born,
Where the three-layered drum,
Bronze mouth, tight leather skin,
The Korybantes beat,

Beat in rhythmic dance,
To the whistle and pipe of flutes.
Mother Earth takes up the beat;
Her worshippers shriek joy,
Shriek joy. Then satyrs snatch the beat;
They dance and dance,
His festival, his,
He smiles, Dionysos!

Sweet in the hills, dance done, race done,
We plunge fulfilled to earth,
We're fawns! We're fawns!
Drink blood, goat's blood,
Raw flesh we eat, joy, joy.

To the hills, to Phrygia, Lydia,
Lord Dionysos lead us! Evohi!
Earth runs with milk, wine, honey –
God-priest lifts high the torch –
Sweet smoke, sweet incense –
He runs, he races, dances –
Goads stragglers,
Dance, dance, evohi,
Hair streaming in the wind,
He sings his Maenads on:

Come Bacchae,
Bacchae, dance.
From golden Tmolos, dance.
Praise Dionysos. Sing.
Beat drums, squeal flutes.
Eveea, evohi. Shout his praise.

To the peaks, the peaks.
Foals we are, foals
In green fields frisking,
Leaping,
For Dionysos, Dionysos.

Dance. Enter TEIRESIAS, *dressed as a Bacchant.*

TEIRESIAS.

Who's on guard? Call Kadmos out,
Agenor's son, who quit Sidon's city
And came here to build towering Thebes.
Go in, fetch him. Say Teiresias wants him.
He knows what I've come about –
His business too. An old man with an older,
We've agreed to dress in fawnskins,
Carry the thyrsos, wear ivy crowns.

Enter KADMOS, *dressed as a Bacchant.*

KADMOS.

My dear old friend, I was inside
And heard your voice – wise man, wise words!
I hurried out, ready, dressed for God.
It's right! We must! My daughter's son,
Dionysos, has revealed himself as God –
We owe him all praise, all honour.
Where shall we dance? Where stamp our feet?
Where shake grey heads? Tell me, Teiresias:
I'm old, you're old, but you're the one who knows.
I'll not grow tired. All day, all night,
I'll thump my thyrsos on the ground –
How sweet it is to dance, to forget old age!

TEIRESIAS.
  You feel as I do – like a boy again,
  Thrilling to the dance.

KADMOS.
  No carriage to take us to the mountain?

TEIRESIAS.
  – and show disrespect for God?

KADMOS.
  Shall I lead the way, old helping old?

TEIRESIAS.
  Leave that to God. He'll help us both.

KADMOS.
  Are we the only ones in Thebes to dance?

TEIRESIAS.
  The only ones to see; the rest are blind.

KADMOS.
  We'd better start. Here, take my hand.

TEIRESIAS.
  Two horses in harness. Off we go!

KADMOS.
  I'm mortal. It's not for me to sneer at gods.

TEIRESIAS.
  No mortal mind can comprehend the gods.
  Religious traditions – ancestral,

Old as time itself, beyond argument:
Prove what you may, they're proof against it.
Are we really such fools, two daft old men
In ivy crowns, popping off to join the dance?
God makes no distinction: dance old,
Dance young, dance one, dance all.
Equal honour from all and none exempt –
That's his demand.

KADMOS.

Teiresias, you're blind (except for second sight) –
I'll see for you, prophesy who's coming.
It's Pentheus, Echion's son, King Pentheus,
The man I gave my throne. What a state he's in!
What's the matter? Does he bring bad news?

Enter PENTHEUS, *with* GUARDS.

PENTHEUS.

As soon as I leave the city, trouble flares!
Some . . . epidemic of nonsense invades all Thebes.
They're leaving home, the women, skipping to the
    woods,
Tripping off to the hills in bogus ecstasy!
They're dancing in homage to the latest fad –
Dionysos, whoever he may be! They say there's more:
Wine-jugs, brimming beside the dancers' feet,
Our women slipping off on the quiet, one by one,
To whore with men. Divine service, they call it;
Priestesses they say they are; it's holy work.
They worship lust, not God.
As many as I found, I rounded up and jailed.

Guards; chains; the cells are crammed.
Some got away, I'll hunt them down.
Away in the hills – my own mother, Agave,
Her sisters, Ino, Autonoe –
I'll soon have them in irons as well.
This nonsense will stop, and smartly.
They say some stranger came smarming into Thebes –
Some magician, some fancy-man from Lydia –
Golden curls, perfumed ringlets, bangs –
Sex dancing in his eyes. A charmer!
They say he's at it with the girls,
Dangling his mysteries all day, all night.
I'll have him. I'll have him here, inside.
Thyrsos-waving! Tossing his lovely locks!
I'll have his head.
They say he's calling Dionysos God –
Stitched up by Zeus in his own royal thigh.
Dionysos! He was charred by a thunderbolt –
His mother too, for slandering Zeus
And saying he slept with her. Blasphemy!
Humbug! Whoever he is, he's earned the noose.

Oh look, another miracle!
Teiresias the star-gazer, in a dappled skin,
And my own grandfather beside him,
Playing Bacchants with their little sticks!
I'm sorry, grandad, it's embarrassing –
Men of your age losing what wits they had.
Unwind that ivy. Give me that stick.
Your idea, presumably, Teiresias?
New gods drum up new trade?
Read the future in some feathered guts

Then burn the bird for God? For cash!
I indulge your age, old man. If you were younger –
chains,
Like all the rest of them. You encouraged these . . .
These orgies. Women and wine don't mix.
Women and wine! What good ever came from that?

CHORUS.
Shame on you, sir. The gods . . .
Your grandfather, who sowed the dragon's teeth . . .
Your own family, my lord! Show more respect.

TEIRESIAS.
If you're clever with words and take your chance,
It's no great thing to make smart remarks.
You've a glib enough tongue, you seem
To make sense, but you don't, you talk nonsense –
And a powerful speaker who's also a fool
Makes nothing but trouble, nothing.
This new God, the one you mock –
I can't describe his growing power
In Greece. My dear boy, two gifts
Are vital to human life. The first
Comes from Demeter, Mother Earth, she has many
names:
The staff of life, our daily bread.
And now the son of Semele gives wine,
To ease our hearts, to soothe our cares.
Drink deep the blood of the vine,
Forget your cares, shed weariness, sleep well.
Gods drink this God in mortal offerings;
Through him all human life is blessed.

You make fun of him? 'Stitched up in Zeus' thigh'?
You profane a sacred mystery.
Zeus snatched him from the lightning-flare,
A new-born child, and carried him on high.
Then Hera, queen of heaven, threatened to throw the
   child
From Sky to Earth. Zeus thwarted her –
When the king of the gods makes plans, who can
   resist?
He took air, the air that enfolds the Earth,
Moulded a child of it, a phantom, and gave it her.
The real child he sent away to safety –
And mortals later made a myth of it.

This God reveals the future, too. The madness
He inspires, the frenzy – prophetic states.
His spirit comes and swamps the flesh,
Presents the future on the drunkard's tongue.
Or he may change and take up Ares' work.
An army's drawn up, standing to arms;
Terror strikes before a spear is raised,
Men break and run – wild Dionysos' work.
You'll see him soon on Delphi's peaks,
Torches flaring on Parnassos' horns,
Brandishing, hurling the ivy-spear.
He'll lord it in Greece. Believe me, Pentheus.
You claim unchallenged power, all power in Thebes.
You're wrong, your confidence is sick, misplaced.
God's here on Earth:
Welcome him, put on his ivy-crown and dance!
You want him to teach our women purity?
In him they find their own pure selves.

See them as they are. The pure in heart
Can dance his dance, their purity untouched.
My lord, you thrill when crowds appear
To line the streets and cheer when Pentheus comes.
God thrills to homage too.
So Kadmos and I, laugh as you will,
Must put on ivy and join the dance –
Greybeards, one two, one two, tread our measure!
Your 'reasons' are delirium. No drug
Can cure it, though drugs may be its cause.
So make what points you will, I'll not fight God.

CHORUS.

Wise words, old man. Apollo's servant, and still
You honour Dionysos, blest be his name.

KADMOS.

Dear boy, what he says is right.
Come with us. Some laws rule even kings.
You argue, you think you think – you don't!
But even if, as you say, he's not a God,
What of it? Politics, Pentheus!
A little lie, a noble lie:
Say Semele's son was God – whose family stands
    to gain?
Remember your cousin Aktaion, his bloody fate,
In a green meadow, savaged to death
By hounds he'd reared himself – and why?
For disparaging Artemis, goddess of the hunt.
God spare you that. Let me crown you, here.
Join us, worship God with us.

PENTHEUS.

Take your hands off me! Go dancing if you must,
But leave me untouched by this . . . this mindlessness.
As for your tutor here, who made you mad,
He'll feel my justice.

To GUARDS:

You! You! Go now
To the platform of prophecy, the place
Where Lord Teiresias plays guessing games –
Pitch it out, the whole contraption, smash it,
Scatter his trappings to the winds.
These teeth can bite! The rest of you,
Scour Thebes, hunt him down, that freak, that foreigner.
He pollutes our women, makes whores of them.
Catch him; chain him; fetch him. Death by stoning!
He'll dance in Thebes all right – the dance of death.

Exit.

TEIRESIAS.

Fool! You've lost all reason now.
It was peevishness before; it's madness now.
We'll go, Kadmos – and as we go we'll pray for him,
Vindictive as he is, pray God's mercy on him, on
Thebes.
Pick up your thyrsos. Walk beside me.
Give me your arm; I'll give you mine –
We're old; for shame if we trip and fall.
We give ourselves to God: Dionysos, son of Zeus.
Pentheus! Pain!

May he bring no grief to you or yours,
Kadmos. No professional prophecies there:
Facts are facts. Only fools say foolish things.

Exeunt.

CHORUS.
    Reverence, god of gods,
    Reverence, who flies on golden wings
    Over the Earth,
    Do you hear Pentheus now,
    Hear his blasphemies
    Against Dionysos, Semele's son,
    Whom blissful gods first toast
    At banquets in their happiness?
    The Roaring Boy,
    He leads the world's dance
    In laughter, the pipe of flutes,
    When wine is poured, flows free
    At the banquets of the gods,
    And when mortals revel, ivy-crowned,
    As the wine-cup gentles their hearts
    And brings them ease.

    Put a bridle on your tongue.
    Irreverence, challenge –
    The end is misery.
    Accept, and nothing can touch you,
    Nothing hurt your house.
    Gods may be far away,
    Mansioned in Sky above,
    But still they look down

And see what mortals do.
Witless! To presume to pass
The bounds of mortal thought.
Human life is brief:
Reach for the impossible,
You'll lose what's in your grasp.
There madness lies;
Fools tread that path,
I say, *I* say.

I dream of Cyprus
Aphrodite's island,
Home of the spirits of love
That seduce all mortal hearts;
Of Paphos, where the hundred mouths
Of distant Nile
Swell the land with crops
That need no rain;
Pieria, most beautiful of all,
Olympos' sacred slopes,
The Muses' home.
Dionysos, O take me there,
Evohi, Dionysos, lord!
There the Graces; there sharp Desire;
There dance is law,
And all must celebrate.

Our guardian-spirit, son of Zeus,
Delights in celebration –
Loves ease-bearing Peace
Who guards our young men's lives.
To rich and poor alike

He gives his wine,
The painless joy.
He despises those
Who disdain such things,
Who by day, by night
Kick away life's joy.
Such arrogance!
Away! Away!
Ours be the common good,
The common way,
The way that all can share.

Enter GUARDS *with* DIONYSOS *bound. Enter*
PENTHEUS.

GUARD COMMANDER.
  My lord, he's here. We hunted him down.
  You ordered it, and here he is.
  Oh, he was easy, didn't run.
  For a wild man, he's pretty tame,
  Held out his hands and came along –
  No resistance, no trouble, cool as you like.
  He helped us chain him, never lost that smile.
  That bothered me. 'I'm just doing my job,' I said.
  'Obeying orders. Lord Pentheus asked for this.'

  Another thing. The women you arrested,
  Chained up and locked in the common jail –
  They're free, dancing in the fields
  In honour of the Roaring Boy, their God.
  The chains fell off themselves –
  No human hand! – the bolts slid back.

He's brought us miracles, my lord.
Miracles. And here he is: all yours.

PENTHEUS.

Let go. He's in the bag.
He can't skip free. He's mine.
Such a fine young fellow! Such a ladies' man!
Is *that* why you came to Thebes? Such hair!
He was never a wrestler.
Look where it hugs his cheek. So sexy!
Soft white skin, no sunburn –
Must use a parasol. Or stay indoors.
This pretty boy likes indoor sports.
Right. Answer. Name? Where from?

DIONYSOS.

So far, so easy.
You've heard of Tmolos, where flowers grow?

PENTHEUS.

Mountain-range. Rings Sardis. Right?

DIONYSOS.

That's where I'm from. A Lydian.

PENTHEUS.

So why bring your mumbo jumbo here?

DIONYSOS.

Dionysos entered me. The son of Zeus.

PENTHEUS.

Some local Zeus is that, who spawns new gods?

DIONYSOS.
    There's only one. He bedded Semele. Right here.

PENTHEUS.
    Did he – ah – enter you – by day or in the dark?

DIONYSOS.
    Face to face he grants his mysteries.

PENTHEUS.
    These mysteries: describe them.

DIONYSOS.
    They're not for unbelievers' ears.

PENTHEUS.
    And believers – what good are they to *them*?

DIONYSOS.
    A fine secret – and one you'll never know.

PENTHEUS.
    Oh, very clever! You whet my appetite.

DIONYSOS.
    God hates whoever mocks his rites.

PENTHEUS.
    This god, you've seen him face to face? What's he like?

DIONYSOS.
    He chooses. It's not for me to say.

PENTHEUS.
  Words! Words! There's nothing there.

DIONYSOS.
  All wisdom sounds like folly to a fool.

PENTHEUS.
  You've tried this . . . gospel somewhere else?

DIONYSOS.
  The whole world dances, all but Greece.

PENTHEUS.
  Only Greece has sense.

DIONYSOS.
  In this, not so. It's a different world.

PENTHEUS.
  Are your . . . services by day or night?

DIONYSOS.
  Night, mostly. Darkness breeds devotion.

PENTHEUS.
  – breeds women's tricks and wiles.

DIONYSOS.
  There are tricks and wiles by day as well.

PENTHEUS.
  Be clever with me, you'll pay for it.

DIONYSOS.
It's you mocks God. There's a price for that as well.

PENTHEUS.
So full of answers! So well prepared!

DIONYSOS.
Tell me my punishment. What terrors lie in store?

PENTHEUS.
Your pretty hair: I'll have it cropped.

DIONYSOS.
It's sacred. I wear it for the God.

PENTHEUS.
After which, give up your thyrsos.

DIONYSOS.
You take it. I carry it for God.

PENTHEUS.
And after that, we'll lock you up.

DIONYSOS.
He'll set me free, whenever I choose.

PENTHEUS.
You'll stand there with your girls and shout for him?

DIONYSOS.
He's here, here now. He sees what you do to me.

PENTHEUS.
Oh? Where exactly? I see no one. Where?

DIONYSOS.
With me. You're blind to God. Your eyes don't see.

PENTHEUS.
Chain him! He laughs at Thebes; at me.

DIONYSOS.
You can't chain me. You're blind. I warn you.

PENTHEUS.
I chain who I like. I'm master here.

DIONYSOS.
You know nothing. Who are you? *Why* are you?

PENTHEUS.
I'm Pentheus. Agave's child. Echion's son.

DIONYSOS.
Pentheus, pain – the link's been made before.

PENTHEUS.
Take him. The stables – chain him there.
It's black enough: he likes the dark.
Dance there! Dance all you like! And your women,
Your harem, I'll make them slaves.
I'll stop their drumming, their drumming:
I'll set them to spin, weave . . . Slaves!

DIONYSOS.

    I'll go. I'll suffer what Fate decrees, no more.
    As for you, your blasphemy will be repaid.
    Dionysos, whom you deny, will see to that.
    Who ill-treats me lays hands on God.

    The GUARDS *take him out. Exit* PENTHEUS.

CHORUS.

    Blessed river,
    Dirke, water of Thebes,
    Pure daughter of Acheloös
    The river god,
    You cradled Dionysos once,
    In your welling pools,
    The son of Zeus.
    His father then −
    Zeus, creator −
    Snatched him up
    From undying fire,
    Flame of the thunderbolt.
    'Come, twice-born, come,
    Inside my thigh,
    The father's womb;
    Be born again,
    Dionysos, Dionysos,
    Name of Names for Thebes.'

    Blessed Dirke,
    Then you welcomed him.
    Why now, now, when he comes
    In garlands, in joy,
    Do you flinch from him,

Deny his name?
Why abuse me?
Why turn away?
By the purple power,
Power of the grape,
You *must* believe –
Dionysos!

What rage he shows, what rage,
Pentheus, Echion's son,
Son of the dragon-seed,
Earth-born! A dragon now,
A giant, no mortal,
Blood-raw, makes war on God.
He nets us, binds us,
God's holy ones, who dance
For the Roaring Boy.
In darkness now he's chained:
My fellow-worshipper,
My dancer, in darkness chained.

Dionysos, son of Zeus.
See how we suffer,
Who call your name.
Come down from Olympos,
Come down to us.
Golden thyrsos high,
In glory, come!
Violence! Blasphemy!
Come and end them now.

Where are you, Dionysos?
On mountain peaks, beasts' lairs,

Thyrsos erect, erect,
As you lead the dance?
In Olympos' leafy haunts,
Where Orpheus' lute brought dance
To trees, made choirs of beasts?
Pieria! He honours you,
Our lord, lord of the dance –
Leads his Bacchants,
His dancers, whirl over rivers,
Axios, father Lydias
Fountain of life,
Where stallions prance,
Prance on fertile soil.

DIONYSOS (*inside*).
    Eeoh!
    Hear me, hear me.
    Eeoh Bacchae, eeoh Bacchae!

CHORUS.
    Who is it? Where?
    Has he come? Up, up,
    Evohi.

DIONYSOS (*inside*).
    Eeoh, eeoh!
    Again I call,
    The son of Semele, the son of Zeus.

CHORUS.
    Eeoh, eeoh, lord,
    Come, Dionysos, come.

DIONYSOS (*inside*).
　Shake, tremble,
　Mother Earth now shake!

Earthquake.

CHORUS.
　Ah, ah.
　Crumble palace, throne fall,
　Dionysos is here.
　Bow, bow. We bow.
　Roof, pillars,
　It cracks, it falls,
　It's down.
　Hear, Dionysos,
　From darkest dungeon hear
　The victory cry.

DIONYSOS (*inside*).
　Crack lightning, flare,
　Gorge on this palace, gorge.

CHORUS.
　Ah, ah.
　Fire, fire.
　The shrine of Semele, all fire.
　God's fire, Zeus' holy fire.
　Kneel, Maenads, kneel.
　The king has come.
　The palace his toy –
　It's up, it's down! –
　The son of Zeus!

Enter DIONYSOS.

DIONYSOS.
Women of the East, what makes you so afraid?
Why do you grovel? You felt Dionysos:
Pentheus' palace in his grasp.
Stand up. Rejoice. Put off your fear.

CHORUS.
Light. Joy. Dionysos.
With us! Our dreams come true.

DIONYSOS.
When he dungeoned me, Pentheus,
When he chained me in darkness, did you despair?

CHORUS.
How could we not?
With you defenceless, who was our defence?
He held you, the blasphemer,
The atheist. How did you escape?

DIONYSOS.
Easily. No effort. I chose – and I was free.

CHORUS.
But you were caged.

DIONYSOS.
He thought so. Chains, shackles –
It wasn't me he caged. He fed on hope like grass.
There was a bull, close by the breeding pens.
Its knees he looped, its hoofs lassooed –
He panted with rage, he sweated, he bit his lips;

I sat at my ease and watched –
And at that very moment God came, the Roaring Boy,
Upended the palace, fire blazing in the shrine.
His Majesty saw it. 'Fire, oh fire!' he shrieked;
Ran up and down; 'Water! Rivers of water! Now!'
Slaves jumped to it – no use, no use.
Then he thought I'd escaped, I'd slipped away.
He dropped that job, grabbed a sword and ran inside.
And there, in the courtyard – or so I think,
I tell only what I think –
God sent a phantom, my double, for him to fight.
He sliced the brilliant air
And thought to cut me down. Dionysos' work!
The god humiliated him, one, two, three!
His palace in the dirt, his life in shreds,
My fetters laughing in the dust.
He dropped his sword. Exhausted, spent:
A mortal who duelled with God. I left him there
And slipped out here to you. What's Pentheus now?
Who cares? No, listen: boots. He's coming.
Now what will he say? Shout fury? Roar?
I'll hear him. Good temper, calm. I'm in control.

Enter PENTHEUS.

PENTHEUS.
Outrage! To me! To me! He's got away,
The stranger caught, chained . . .

E-a! E-a!
I've got him! Here! Outrageous!
He's standing here, outside my house!

DIONYSOS.

That's enough. Stop fretting. Calm.

PENTHEUS.

You were chained. Inside. How did you escape?

DIONYSOS.

I told you – didn't you hear? – that *he* would free me.

PENTHEUS.

Who? Another mystery! Who?

DIONYSOS.

He who gives mortals the tendrils of the vine.

PENTHEUS.

– to make fools of them, to drive them mad.

DIONYSOS.

Your words, my lord. You sneer at God.

PENTHEUS.

Guards! Bar the gates. No one in or out.

DIONYSOS.

D'you think the gods can't vault your gates?

PENTHEUS.

You've an answer for everything. We'll see!

DIONYSOS.

I see what I see. I know what I know.

Now, listen to this man:
A cowherd from the hills, with news.
I'll wait till you want me. I won't run away.

Enter COWHERD.

COWHERD.
Majesty, Pentheus,
I come from Kithairon,
The high peaks, where driven snow –

PENTHEUS.
If this is important, tell it.

COWHERD.
I saw the holy ones, the dancers,
Spear-swift, swarming, white-naked.
My lord, I come to tell you – tell the city –
The wonders they do – beyond belief.
Shall I trim my words, Majesty, or tell it plain?
I'm afraid. Your temper, lord. Kings snap; they bite.

PENTHEUS.
Speak out. An honest man
Has nothing to fear from me. But them!
The worse your story, the worse for him,
Who put these women up to it.

COWHERD.
I was with my herds, Majesty,
Working them to high pasture. Just after dawn:
Sun's rays like spears, to warm the Earth.

I saw them, the women, three groups of them,
Their leaders Autonoe, Ino and Agave your mother.
They were asleep, bodies tumbled together,
Pillowed on pine needles, oak-leaves,
The bare ground. They lay where they were,
Relaxed, innocent − not drunk with wine or music,
As you warned us, lord, not whoring among the trees.
All at once, my cattle lowed. One . . . another . . .
Your mother woke with a cry,
Jumped up and called the others.
They shook sleep from their eyes, stood up,
Erect, refreshed, in beauty clean −
Young women, old, unmarried girls.
Their hair fell loose about their shoulders.
They fastened their fawnskins where they'd slipped
     undone,
The fastenings living snakes, that licked their cheeks.
Some cradled fawns, or wolf-cubs,
Offered them white breasts
Pearling with milk from babies left behind.
Others plaited crowns to wear:
Ivy, oak-leaves, flowering briony.
One took a thyrsos, struck the rock −
Water sprang. Another jabbed the ground −
A spurt of wine, God's gift.
For milk they stroked the stones: it flowed.
Sweet honey dripped from thyrsos down.
My lord, if you'd been there and seen such things,
The god you now abuse would see you on your knees.

We herdsmen, shepherds, all of us there,
Fell over each other, trying to make sense

Of all the wonders. One of us –
Hot from the city, he'd heard the talk –
Said, 'Mountain-men, friends, listen.
Suppose we round Agave up, his lordship's mother,
Take her out of the dance?
He'd be grateful then, his Majesty. Wouldn't he?'
A smart idea. We hid in the bushes
And waited for our chance. At last it came.
The dance began – the swaying, the thyrsos,
'Dionysos, Iacchos!' Beasts, mountains,
All together in the world's great dance.
Nearer she came, Agave, nearer, nearer . . .
The ambush, I make a grab, she screams:
'Run, hounds, run! They're after us –
Men, hunters, run them down –
The thyrsos – arm yourselves and hunt them down.'
We ran for it. They'd have torn us in pieces!
Our cattle were stranded. On a patch of green,
With bare white hands the women fell on them.
One lifts a whole heifer as it bellows,
Tears it in two! Others dismember calves –
Ribs, hooves, hurtling in the air,
The pines bow down with bleeding flesh –
And the bulls! Glorious with angry horns,
Down, down they go – hands, girl's hands,
Hundreds of hands, strip flesh from bones –
Before you could blink, your Majesty!
Off then, like a flock of birds,
Skimming, swooping to the water-meadows,
Asopos' stream, the ripening corn
Below the crags, the villages, they plunged
Like enemies and fell on them.

Panic and plunder! Babies snatched from homes
Go riding on their shoulders, easy,
Balanced safe above the nightmare.
Nothing stops them – bronze, iron, fire –
They wear flames for ribbons in their hair!
Furious villagers run to arms –
And then, oh then, my lord –
Their spearpoints draw no blood!
But when the thyrsos flies, the ivy-point,
Blood spurts. Men turned and ran;
Women routed men. Thanks be to God. All right.
Then up to the heights they swarmed again.
To the water-springs God blessed them with.
Washed away the blood, while snakes
Licked clean their gory cheeks.

This god, sir, whoever he is –
Make him welcome. His power. His force.
The gift of wine gives pause to pain.
Lord, banish wine, all pleasure's lost,
All love, the joy of life – all gone.

CHORUS.
Pardon me, Majesty. I speak my mind.
I must. Dionysos is God,
None greater. His name be praised.

PENTHEUS.
So. It's here. This fire, this dancing,
This craze that degrades all Greece.
No time to waste. To the gates, now,
Spearmen, archers, horsemen.

Death to the Bacchae. The shame of it –
To be defied by women and not fight back!

DIONYSOS.

You've ears and hear nothing.
You ill-treat me, Pentheus, and still I warn you:
Disarm. Do nothing to injure God.
Resign yourself. The Roaring Boy
Will never see his dancers down
From the hills, the peaks of joy.

PENTHEUS.

Be quiet. You've escaped so far –
Or do you want more punishment?

DIONYSOS.

Better pray than prate.
You're mortal. You can't fight God.

PENTHEUS.

Prey, you say? I'll prey on them, the women,
Drown every glen, every stream, with blood.

DIONYSOS.

You'll run before them, all of you.
The thyrsos will rape your shields.

PENTHEUS.

Immigrant, you'll be the death of me!
In chains, set free, you won't shut up.

DIONYSOS.

My dear, there's a simple way to handle this –

PENTHEUS.
Which is . . . ? Play slave to slaves?

DIONYSOS.
I'll get them here. No need of force.

PENTHEUS.
Oee moee. Now what – another trick?

DIONYSOS.
No trick. My powers can save you.

PENTHEUS.
A plot to keep the dance alive.

DIONYSOS.
Plot, yes – and it's working out. God knows.

PENTHEUS (*to a* GUARD).
Fetch my armour.

To DIONYSOS:

And you, shut up.

DIONYSOS.
Ssss.
D'you want to see them at it, in the hills?

PENTHEUS.
See them? More than gold I'd give . . .

DIONYSOS.
    What, most of all? What . . . turns you on?

PENTHEUS.
    I'd shudder to see them drunk.

DIONYSOS.
    Delicious pain. It stings, and still you want – ?

PENTHEUS.
    I could hide in the trees and watch –

DIONYSOS.
    If you hide, they'll sniff you out.

PENTHEUS.
    You're right. I'll go there openly.

DIONYSOS.
    We'll go together. You mean what you say?

PENTHEUS.
    I mean it. Now! Don't waste my time.

DIONYSOS.
    First, then, my lord: a woman's dress.

PENTHEUS.
    A dress? I'm to change my sex?

DIONYSOS.
    If you go as a man, you're dead.

PENTHEUS.
    Right again. You think of everything.

DIONYSOS.
    I think what Dionysos thinks, no more.

PENTHEUS.
    How can it be done, what you propose?

DIONYSOS.
    I'll see to it. I'll dress you. Come inside.

PENTHEUS.
    In women's clothes? How can I?

DIONYSOS.
    You wanted to see them . . . to watch them dance?

PENTHEUS.
    This dress – you'll help me?

DIONYSOS.
    Your hair, first. I'll make it long.

PENTHEUS.
    And then? What then?

DIONYSOS.
    A full-length dress . . . a veil.

PENTHEUS.
    What else?

DIONYSOS.
  A fawnskin . . . a thyrsos . . .

PENTHEUS.
  I can't put on women's clothes. I can't.

DIONYSOS.
  You'd rather fight them? Blood on blood?

PENTHEUS.
  Better see what they're up to first?

DIONYSOS.
  Much better. First gather your evidence.

PENTHEUS.
  I can get through Thebes and not be seen?

DIONYSOS.
  There are lonely streets. I know a way.

PENTHEUS.
  I won't be laughed at. They mustn't laugh.
  I'll go in now . . . I'll think it through.

DIONYSOS.
  Do that. Whatever you decide, I'm here.

PENTHEUS.
  Two choices: to go in arms,
  Or . . . do as you suggest.

Exit.

DIONYSOS.
Women, he's caught!
He'll comes to the Bacchae, and die for it.
Dionysos, you're here, this is in your hands.
Punish him. Possess him, dizzy him.
In his right mind, he'll never wear women's clothes;
Let madness slip the reins – he'll do it!
I'll make him the laughing-stock of Thebes –
His Majesty in drag, who tried to make me tremble.
I'll go in now, I'll help him dress,
His bridal robes, for honeymoon in Hell –
His own mother's hands will see to that.
He'll learn. He'll learn.
Dionysos, true son of Zeus, brings double gifts:
Raw punishment, and sweet rewards.

Exit.

CHORUS.
Soon we'll dance –
White feet, ecstatic night,
Neck arched, dew falls,
Fawns in a playful meadow,
Thrilling green,
From the hunters free,
From throbbing fear,
Leap plaited nets,
The hunters' whoop,
Dogs run and run.
Leap free,

Skip windswift,
Water-meadows,
Pleasure of lonely woods –
No men, no men! –
In secret shade.

Wisdom? What's that?
What truer gift from God
Than hands outstretched
In triumph above your enemy?
Revenge is sweet, they say.

Slowly it comes,
In God's good time, believe it.
God's punishment
For mortals,
Their folly, their craziness,
Who worship Vanity above the gods.
Along they come, the gods,
Down the passages of time,
Blasphemers their prey.
Old ways are best.
Observe. Revere.
How little it costs:
Allow them power, the gods –
As it was in the beginning –
The Law is the Law –
All Nature proves it so.

Wisdom? What's that?
What truer gift from God
Than hands outstretched

In triumph above your enemy?
Revenge is sweet, they say.

Happy those who out of storm
Find shelter,
Who out of toil
Find rest.
They race –
The one, the other,
This way, that way,
Wealth, power, the winner!
A thousand hearts, a thousand hopes.
Some make it – success, success! –
Others fade away.
I say: accept what comes.
Live day by day.
Be calm. Be happy.

Enter DIONYSOS.

DIONYSOS.
    You.
    So hot to see what should not be seen,
    To do what should not be done.
    Pentheus, come out.
    In public, show me:
    Women's clothes, a Bacchant.
    All set to spy on mother and her crew.
    You'll be one of Kadmos' daughters yet!

Enter PENTHEUS, *dressed as a woman Bacchant.*

PENTHEUS.

Two suns I see. I think I see.
Two cities. Two seven-mouthed walls.
You lead me. Bull. You've horns.
Were you bull before? Bull now.

DIONYSOS.

God leads you. Smiles, who frowned before.
All for you now. You see what you must see.

PENTHEUS.

Do I walk like them, look like them —
Like Ino, like Agave my mother?

DIONYSOS.

When I look at you, I think I see them.
There's a curl, here, out of place.
I tucked it behind your veil.

PENTHEUS.

I shook it loose when I rehearsed, inside.
I danced for God. I danced it free.

DIONYSOS.

Lift your head. I'm here to help.
I'll see to you.

PENTHEUS.

There. See. I'm in your hands.

DIONYSOS.

Your belt's too loose. The folds of your dress
Should fall straight to the ankle.

PENTHEUS.

That's right. This side's all wrong.
This side's perfect; straight to the heel.

DIONYSOS.

You'll call me the best of friends.
Sober ecstasy you'll see, not orgies as you suppose.

PENTHEUS.

Which hand for the thyrsos – this, or this?
What should a proper dancer do?

DIONYSOS.

The right. Right foot, right hand –
Up! Hah! I'm glad to see you . . . changed.

PENTHEUS.

If I chose, I could lift them all –
All the dancers, all Kithairon. Bend, and lift –

DIONYSOS.

If you chose. You were blind before;
Now you see . . . as you ought to see.

PENTHEUS.

Shall I lever them up, the peaks?
Or with these bare hands attack them, rip them?

DIONYSOS.

Leave them standing. Mountain nymphs dance there,
Pan pipes . . .

PENTHEUS.

You're right. No violence. They're women.
No need of force. I'll hide among the trees.

DIONYSOS.

You'll have your hiding.
You'll play your trick.
You'll see them dance.

PENTHEUS.

I'll have them like birds in the bushes,
Snared in love's honey-trap.

DIONYSOS.

That's why you're going: to catch them at it,
Unless they catch you first.

PENTHEUS.

Take me there . . . through the city . . .
For this, I'm the only man in Thebes.

DIONYSOS.

The only one. You take this on alone.
Your ordeal, your destiny. Come, now.
I'll see you there. No harm on the way.
Another's hands will bring you home.

PENTHEUS.

My mother.

DIONYSOS.

You'll be carried high.

PENTHEUS.
   As I deserve.

DIONYSOS.
   In mother's arms.

PENTHEUS.
   She'll cradle me.

DIONYSOS.
   For all to see.

PENTHEUS.
   She'll spoil me so.

DIONYSOS.
   Spoiled you shall be.

PENTHEUS.
   My destiny!

   Exit.

DIONYSOS.
   You'll make all mortals tremble.
   Such fame, such suffering, a tower of pain.
   Agave, daughters of Kadmos, stretch out your hands!
   He's coming. The battle is now.
   For Dionysos, Roaring Boy, cry victory!
   The future is now, is now.

   Exit.

CHORUS.

Run,
Hounds of madness, run.
To the hills, to the dance.
The daughters of Kadmos: prick them,
Stampede them against that spy,
That madman in women's clothes.
His mother first to spot him –
In smooth rocks lurking,
Among the trees, he's there!
She'll warn the dancers:
'A man! A man!
From Thebes he comes; he spies on us;
Who is he, who?
No woman gave him birth:

A lioness, a Gorgon,
A monster from the East.'

Justice, snatch the knife,
Stab, stab
The godless one,
Dragon-seed, Earth-spawn,
The lawless one.

Wrong!
Unjust! Insane!
He foams, he frets, he roars.
'I'll end the dance, end it,
I'll conquer God!' God conquers all.
The way to mortal happiness,
Lives free of pain, is this:
Be humble, revere the gods.

Let the clever be clever,
Good luck to them.
There's another road, another,
Leads wide to joy:
Day and night respect the gods,
Honour them,
Reject injustice and honour God.

Justice, snatch the knife,
Stab, stab
The godless one,
Dragon-seed, Earth-spawn,
The lawless one.

Dionysos, come!
Show yourself: bull,
Hundred-headed snake,
Lion snorting flame.
Dionysos, come!
He hunts your dancers –
After him!
Wreathe him with smiles,
Net him, trample him,
Women, dance him down.

Dance. Enter ATTENDANT.

ATTENDANT.
    This palace once stood for happiness:
    Home of Kadmos, who sowed the dragon-seed.
    Now your summer's gone. I weep for you.
    A slave, and still I weep.

CHORUS.
What's happened? The dancers? Speak!

ATTENDANT.
Pentheus is dead, Echion's son.

CHORUS.
Dionysos, god of gods, you're here!

ATTENDANT.
What d'you mean? Woman!
Our master's dead, and you make songs?

CHORUS.
I sing as I like. He's dead.
No punishment now, no chains.

ATTENDANT.
You think no men are left, no men in Thebes?

CHORUS.
Dionysos, not Thebes, commands me now.

ATTENDANT.
Even so . . . such suffering, and still you gloat.

CHORUS.
Tell me. Spell it out. How did he die,
That tyrant, that criminal, that . . . man?

ATTENDANT.
We left the last farms on the Theban plain,

Crossed the river and made for the mountain,
Pentheus and I – I attended his Majesty –
And that stranger who took us to . . .
What we were to see. We were in a grassy gully,
Huddled down, feet still, tongues still –
We'd come to see, not be seen. On each side, rocks.
A stream running past. Overarching pines.
And there they were! The women. Sitting, busy –
Simple tasks, ordinary. There was ivy loose
On a thyrsos tip – they bound it tight again.
Some were singing. Frisky . . . foals set free.
Happy songs, holy songs, God-songs.
Pentheus, he was doomed, he couldn't see them.
'Stranger,' he said, 'Where are they? The dancers?
I can't see from here. If I was higher,
If I climbed a tree, I'd see every detail,
I'd see what filth they're at.'
Then, the impossible – the stranger did it.
Took the tip of a pine where it brushed the sky
And bent it down, down to the dark ground.
Arched like a bow, hooped like a perfect curve
Drawn with peg and line – barehanded so
The stranger bent it like a twig,
No mortal feat. Pentheus he perched
High in the branches . . . eased the trunk erect . . .
Gently, steadily, don't twitch him loose.
Up, up it rose, sheer above us to the sky,
His Majesty riding, riding . . .
Did he see them then? Who knows? But they saw him.
No sooner was he there, up there –
I couldn't see the stranger any more –
Than a voice came, Dionysos it must have been,

A voice out of nowhere. 'My dears, he's yours.
He mocked me, God; he mocked my dance,
My mystery. Now punish him.' And with the voice
A flare, a tower of light, from sky to earth.

Silence. Air, rocks, trees, no sound.
No living sound. The women stood there,
Gazing round, puzzled. God's words not clear?
Then the voice again. This time they knew.
Swift as doves they darted, Kadmos' daughters,
His mother, her sisters, the whole pack of them –
Across the torrent, up steep stone slopes,
On fire for God.
And there was Pentheus, squatting in his tree.
They climbed higher up, hurled stones at him,
Pine-twigs, thyrsos-spears. A sitting target –
Trembling – but too high up, perched out of reach.
They found an oak-tree, stripped it,
Made levers of its branches, to uproot the pine.
No use. Then Agave said, 'Stand round it,
Make a circle, take hold of the trunk. We need
This climbing beast, before it tells God's dance.'
A thousand hands take hold. They pluck the tree –
And down comes Pentheus, tumbling, screaming –
Did he know the pain to come?

His mother began the kill.
He snatched off his wig, his veil.
'Don't you know me, mother? It's Pentheus,
Your baby, your little boy.
Don't hurt me, mother. I've been naughty.
Don't kill me.' He tried to touch her cheek,

But her mouth was foam; unseeing eyes rolled white;
Mindless, possessed by God, she knew no other.
She snatched his wrist, his left wrist,
Braced one foot on his ribs,
And tore his arm away. God gave her strength.
Now Ino was at work, the other side,
Tearing, tearing; Autonoe and all the pack.
Noise:
His Majesty screaming while still he'd lungs to scream,
The women shrieking, shrieking.
One carried off an arm; a foot, neat in its boot;
Ribs, stripped white. They made a game of it,
Played catch with lumps of Pentheus' meat.

His carcass is up there still. Everywhere:
The rocks, the undergrowth. Pieces of Pentheus.
The head – poor head –
His mother took it in her hands,
Pronged it on a thyrsos, a trophy,
Carries it in triumph down from the hills.
She's coming now. She left the others, dancing,
And now she's coming here. Singing for joy,
For Dionysos, fellow-hunter, in at the kill:
The victor whose prize is tears.
I won't stay. Won't see. Won't hear.
The world's collapsed. Moderation . . .
Respect for God, but moderation: we need that now.

Exit.

CHORUS.
    Dance for Dionysos, dance.

Sing Pentheus, dead,
Dragon-seed,
Who wore women's clothes,
Clutched the thyrsos,
Clutched his own death,
Bull – led to die, to die.
Women, daughters of Kadmos,
Famous victory is yours –
And tears, and tears.
Sweet horror: a mother's hands
Made crimson cradle for her son.

She's coming, she's here,
Agave, mad-eyed, white-eyed.
Welcome here, welcome.
Evohi! God!

Enter AGAVE, *with* PENTHEUS' *head.*

AGAVE.
Women, dancers, look –

CHORUS.
We see.

AGAVE.
Down from the hills we bring
New vines for the palace,
Cuttings blessed by god.

CHORUS.
We welcome you, the hunt.

AGAVE.
    No snares, I caught him,
    Look! The lion-cub,
    Whelp of the lioness.

CHORUS.
    In what wild place?

AGAVE.
    Kithairon –

CHORUS.
    Kithairon!

AGAVE.
    Did him down.

CHORUS.
    Whose hands?

AGAVE.
    Mine first the joy of it.
    'Agave, blessed!', they sing,
    They dance.

CHORUS.
    Who helped?

AGAVE.
    His children . . . .

CHORUS.
    Whose?

AGAVE.
Kadmos' children, after me, oh after me,
Laid hands on him.
God watched our hunt, smiled down.

Come, join the feast.

CHORUS.
A feast of tears.

AGAVE.
So young a cub, so young.
Baby cheeks, soft fur
Like down on silky mane.

CHORUS.
Like a lion he seems, a lion.

AGAVE.
God's clever, clever in the hunt.
He led; we chased; we danced,
Danced lion dead.

CHORUS.
God hunts.

AGAVE.
Praise him.

CHORUS.
Praise him.

AGAVE.
Soon all Thebes –

CHORUS.
And Pentheus?

AGAVE.
Will praise me: mother, hunter,
Who trapped the lion,
Who killed.

CHORUS.
Fearful.

AGAVE.
Fearful.

CHORUS.
You sing?

AGAVE.
I sing for joy.
It's mine. I did it, I.
My hands. Look here, look here!

CHORUS.
Show us, lady. Show all of Thebes.
Sad lady, show your prize.

AGAVE.
Thebans, proud in your tall-towered town,
Behold this prey. He's ours!

We daughters of Kadmos went wild for him.
No nets, no hunting spears:
With hooks of hands we hunted him.
No cleavers, knives:
White hands, bare hands, we butchered him.

Where's Kadmos, my father? Call him.
Where's Pentheus, my son? Tell him:
Fetch a ladder, a hammer . . .
Big game . . . I'll nail this trophy high.

Enter KADMOS, *with* ATTENDANTS *carrying*
PENTHEUS' *body.*

KADMOS.
    This way, your burden, here.
    Bring what was Pentheus, home.
    As much as we could find, fragments,
    Among the trees, the rocks . . .
    They did it. My daughters did it.
    We were home again in Thebes,
    Teiresias and I, our dancing done.
    A servant came. Out I went again,
    To Kithairon, to fetch him home,
    My child, my boy, death-danced.
    Autonoe was there . . . Ino . . . witless among the trees.
    Agave came here, I'm told,
    Danced here. It's true. I see her.
    Nothing here for smiles.

AGAVE.
    Boast, father, boast.

No man alive has daughters fine as yours!
All fine, all fine, and especially me.
No more women's stuff, no more loom –
I'm a hunter now. I did it. Look!
We'll hang it high on the palace walls.
Take it, father, touch it. Be glad for me, proud.
A feast, a banquet, all invited –
Lucky man, your daughter did such things!

KADMOS.

Such things! See what you did. Grief beyond grief.
You did it. Your own hands did it.
Fine sacrifice to set before the gods,
Fine feast you set for Thebes, for me.
Oee moee, for you, for me.
How just God is! How cruel!
His own people, he's danced us down.

AGAVE.

Who's a sour old man? Why so grumpy?
Why these frowns? I want my son
To lead the hunt, to be like me,
To head the pack. Instead, he makes war on God.
He does. You tell him, father. Explain to him.
Fetch Pentheus, someone. Bring him here
To witness what prize is mine, her Majesty!

KADMOS.

Feoo feoo. Don't ever know
The things you did. No tears.
Stay forever as you are –
Innocent misery, false joy.

AGAVE.
What misery? What tears? Father, what's happened?

KADMOS.
Look up, child. Up at the sky.

AGAVE.
What is it?

KADMOS.
Does it seem the same, or has it changed?

AGAVE.
It's brighter, it's dazzling.

KADMOS.
You were flying. Are you flying still?

AGAVE.
What d'you mean, father? I feel . . .
What's happening?

KADMOS.
Do you understand what I'm saying?
Can you give clear replies?

AGAVE.
What were we saying, father? I forgot.

KADMOS.
Your husband . . . what was his name?

AGAVE.
Echion, of the dragon-seed.

KADMOS.
And *his* son's name? The son you bore him?

AGAVE.
Pentheus.

KADMOS.
Whose . . . head . . . is that?

AGAVE.
A lion's. They said it was, the women, the hunters.

KADMOS.
Look at it. Look.

AGAVE.
E-a. What is it, here in my hands?

KADMOS.
Now you understand.

AGAVE.
What have I done?

KADMOS.
No lion.

AGAVE.
Pentheus. Pain.

KADMOS.
The mourners wailed; you heard none of it.

AGAVE.
Who killed him? How did he . . . ? These hands . . . ?

KADMOS.
Harsh truth – its moment strikes.

AGAVE.
Tell me. My heart thuds. Tell me.

KADMOS.
You killed him. Your sisters and yourself.

AGAVE.
In the palace? Where . . . ?

KADMOS.
Where Aktaion's hounds ripped *him* to death.

AGAVE.
Kithairon! Why should he go there?

KADMOS.
To jeer at God, jeer at God's dancers: you.

AGAVE.
We were on Kithairon?

KADMOS.
All Thebes was dancing. All Thebes, possessed.

AGAVE.
God did us down. Dionysos. Now I see.

KADMOS.

You insulted him before. Denied him.

AGAVE.

And my son's sweet corpse? Father, where?

KADMOS.

I . . . gathered it and brought it here.

AGAVE.

He *shared* my madness?

KADMOS.

Like you, he refused to acknowledge God.
A single ruin now engulfs us all:
Your sisters, you, our whole royal house.
Humiliation, scandal, death.
I had no son and now your son is dead:
My sentinel, pillar of the house,
Hammer of Thebes. I'm old, but none dared mock me.
Your crown was strong, your justice sharp.
Kadmos, once called the great, now outcast:
No place for him who sowed the seed of Thebes
And reaped a glittering harvest.
Of all men I loved you, loved you;
Now, in death, I love you still.
My boy! You're dead.
You'll never again stroke this beard,
Hug me, call me Grandad, say
'Who hurts you, slights you?
Who saddens your heart?
Just say his name, I'll punish him . . . father . . . '

I'm dead. Destroyed. You're dead.
Your mother, her sisters, all destroyed.
Do any here disbelieve in God?
See how he died. Believe.

CHORUS.
My lord, I pity you. He died as he deserved.
He earned his death. But the pain is yours, is yours.

AGAVE.
Father, people of Thebes, you see?
In a little hour all's changed for me:
My happiness horror, my pride despair.
His body, father. I killed my son.
I must lay him out, wash sweet limbs
For burial. Blood of my blood.
How shall I weep for you? Here are tears
From a mother's heart, torn as you were torn.
The head, father. Help me, bring the head.
We must make him pretty, make him decent.
That beloved face. Those downy cheeks.
Mother will dress you. There. There –
Your head, your body raw with blood.
Friends, weep your tears, weep for your king,
For the mother who murdered him.

Enter DIONYSOS *on high.*

DIONYSOS.
Thebans, I return: Dionysos, son of Zeus.
In Thebes, where I was born, I showed myself God –
And this mortal insulted me, chained me.

For which he died. Mother's hands. So much for him.
Now for the rest: the future.
First, this people will be driven out
To wander the world, beggars, slaves,
Till their guilt is cleansed.
Next, Agave and her silly sisters.
You denied me, God. Semele, my mother,
You defamed. You polluted Thebes
With Pentheus' blood. Out with you.
Exile, the price you pay. The law insists:
No murderers shall share
The ground with the one they did to death.

Last, Kadmos. You sowed the serpent seed
And serpent shall you be and . . . crawl.
Your wife, Harmonia Ares' daughter, serpent too.
Bulls then you'll yoke, bulls to your chariot:
Lead armies, a million men, sack cities –
Greek cities, until they rape Apollo's shrine,
And find a bitter homecoming. You'll survive, alone –
For his daughter's sake, lord Ares will rescue you;
With the souls of the blessed at last you'll rest.

The future. Dionysos speaks,
No mortal's child, the son of Zeus.
It might have been otherwise:
You might have prospered,
I might have been on your side.
But you refused.

KADMOS.
    Dionysos, we've sinned, be merciful.

DIONYSOS.
 Your eyes are open now, too late.
 You should have looked before.

KADMOS.
 We're guilty, lord. But this! But this!

DIONYSOS.
 I was yours, and you defied me: God.

KADMOS.
 Show mercy, lord. Leave revenge to mortals.

DIONYSOS.
 My father, Zeus, decreed this long ago.

AGAVE.
 Aee aee. Outcasts we are, condemned.

DIONYSOS,
 It's fate. You can't escape. Go, now.

KADMOS.
 My child, we're ripped apart:
 Your sisters, you, your father. Weep!
 I'm doomed to share my life
 With foreigners, a foreign horde,
 Fight Greeks, serpent with serpent wife.
 Plunder Greek shrines, Greek tombs.
 No end. No rest,
 Till I sail the calming stream of death.

AGAVE.

Father, how can I leave you, go into exile?
I must, I must.

KADMOS.

Don't hug me, child. Don't stroke my hair.
You're a swan, a white swan, cherishing . . .

AGAVE.

My Thebes is dead. Where shall I go?

KADMOS.

I don't know, child. Your father's . . . lost.

AGAVE.

Farewell, my home, my country.
I'm an exile. I've nowhere:
An outcast, who once was queen.

KADMOS.

Go, child.

AGAVE.

I weep for you, father.

KADMOS.

And I for you.
These tears are for you, your sisters.

AGAVE.

How could God do this?
How let us suffer so?

DIONYSOS.
  I suffered. God suffered.
  Disowned in Thebes.

AGAVE.
  Father, farewell.

KADMOS.
  Fare you well, sad daughter.
  Your road is hard.

AGAVE.
  Come, women, come, sisters.
  Desolate exiles, hand in hand.
  No more Kithairon foul.
  No thyrsos now. No memory.
  Let others dance.

  Exit.

CHORUS.
  In heaven, Zeus holds the balance.
  Expect the unexpected.
  What mortals dream, the gods frustrate;
  For the impossible, they find a way.
  The proof is what happened here, today.

  Exeunt.

Glossary and Pronunciation Guide

Stressed syllables are in capital letters.

ACHELOÖS (ach-e-LOH-oss). One of the rivers of Thebes.

AGAVE (A-ga-veh; Greek a-YAH-veh, 'princess'). Kadmos' daughter; Pentheus' mother.

AGENOR (AJ-e-nor, Greek a-YEE-nohr). Mythical father of Kadmos.

AKTAION (ak-TEE-on, Greek AK-te-ohn). Hunter who saw the goddess Artemis bathing, and was punished by being torn to bits by his own dogs.

APHRODITE (af-ro-DIE-tee, Greek af-ro-DEE-teh, 'foam-born'). Goddess of beauty and sexual desire.

APOLLO (a-POL-lo; Greek a-po-LOHN, 'destroyer'). God of sunlight, music, medicine and prophecy.

ARES (AY-rees, Greek AH-rees, 'warrior'). God of war.

ARTEMIS (ar-TEE-miss, Greek AR-te-miss, 'water-spring'). Goddess of hunting and childbirth.

ASOPOS (a-SOH-poss). River on Mount Kithairon.

AUTONOE (ow-TO-no-eh, Greek af-to-NOH-ee, 'mind of her own'). Agave's sister.

AXIOS (AKS-i-oss, ak-SEE-oss). River.

BACCHAE (BAK-kie, Greek VA-cheh, 'revellers'; also known as Bacchants). Dionysos' ecstatic followers.

BAKTRIA (BAK-tri-a, Greek vak-TREE-a). Modern
  Afghanistan.

DELPHI (DEL-fee, Greek thel-FEE). Apollo's shrine on
  the slopes of Mount Parnassos.

DEMETER (dee-MEE-ter, Greek thee-mee-TEER,
  'barley-mother'). Goddess of harvest'; a name for
  Mother Earth.

DIONYSOS (die-on-IE-soss, Greek thee-on-i-SOSS, 'sky-
  shoot' or 'sprig of Zeus'), god of instinct and the
  abandonment of self.

DIRKE (DUR-kee, Greek THEER-keh, 'deep') One of
  the rivers of Thebes.

ECHION (EK-ee-on, Greek e-CHEE-ohn, 'viper').
  Pentheus' father.

EVOHI, EVEEA (yoo-OH-ee, Greek ev-OH-ee; ev-EE-a).
  Ecstatic cries of Dionysos' worshippers.

GORGON (GOR-gon). Monster whose gaze turned flesh
  to stone.

HERA (HEE-ra, Greek EE-ree, 'protector') Goddess of
  oaths and promises (especially marriage-vows); consort
  of Zeus.

IACCHOS (YAK-koss, 'roaring one'). Cult-name for
  Dionysos, shouted by his ecstatic worshippers.

INO (IE-noh, Greek EE-nohn, 'she who makes sinewy').
  Agave's sister.

ISMENOS (is-MAY-noss, Greek EES-mee-noss). One of
  the rivers of Thebes.

KADMOS (KAD-moss, 'man from the East'). Founder of
  Thebes; father of Semele, grandfather of Pentheus and
  Dionysos.

KITHAIRON (kith-IE-ron, Greek kith-i-ROHN).
  Mountain near Thebes.

KORYBANTES (kor-i-BAN-tees, Greek kor-i-VAN-tees, 'crested ones'). Sacred dancers.

KYBELE (KI-be-leh, Greek ki-VEE-leh, 'axe-queen'). Earth-goddess; a name for Mother Earth.

LYDIA (LID-ya, Greek lee-THEE-a). (Modern) Aegean coastal area of Turkey.

LYDIAS (LID-ee-ass, Greek lee-THEE-ass). River.

MAENADS (MEE-nads, Greek MIE-na-des, 'maddened ones'). Ecstatic followers of Dionysos.

OLYMPOS (o-LIM-poss, Greek o-lim-BOSS). Highest mountain in Greece; home of the gods.

ORPHEUS (or-FYOOSS, Greek or-FEVS, 'born on a river-bank'). Apollo's son, moved even rocks, wild beasts and the Dead by his singing.

PAN. God of shepherds, known for his playing of the pan-pipes.

PAPHOS (PAF-oss). Birthplace of Aphrodite in Cyprus.

PARNASSOS (par-NASS-oss, Greek PAR-nass-oss). Twin-peaked mountain-range above Delphi, where Apollo and Dionysos danced with the Muses and their mortal followers.

PENTHEUS (PEN-thyoos, Greek pen-THEFS, '[son of] grief'). Son of Princess Agave and ruler of Thebes.

PHRYGIA (FRIJ-ya, Greek free-YEE-a). (Modern) north-western Turkey.

PIERIA (pie-EE-ri-a, Greek pi-er-EE-a). Mountain where the Muses lived.

SARDIS (SAR-diss, Greek SAR-deess). City in the foothills of Tmolos.

SATYRS (SAY-ters, Greek sa-TEERS). Goat-footed dancers, wood-spirits and followers of Dionysos.

SEMELE (SE-me-leh, Greek see-MEE-lee, 'Moon-princess'). Daughter of Kadmos; mother of Dionysos.

SIDON (SIE-don, Greek see-THOHN). City in Palestine; in Greek myth, the birthplace of Kadmos.

TEIRESIAS (tie-REE-see-ass, Greek ti-ri-SEE-ass, 'who delights in omens'). Blind Theban prophet and seer.

THEBES (THEEBS, Greek THEE-veh). Town in central Greece, founded by Kadmos.

THYRSOS (THUR-soss, Greek THEER-soss). Pine-branch tipped with a pine-cone (real or ornamental) and wound with wisps of wool; pole carried by Dionysos' worshippers.

TMOLOS (TMO-loss). Sacred mountain-range in (modern) central Turkey.

ZEUS (ZYOOS [one syllable, but not 'Zoos', add the 'y' of 'yes']; Greek ZEFS, 'shining sky'). God of the visible universe, ruler of gods and mortals.